THE DIARY OF TERESA DI SCLAFANI

TERESA DI SCLAFANI DE NASCA

TecnoTur
Publishing
Is there a book inside you?

CONTENTS

The Diary of Teresa Di Sclafani

Published by TecnoTur Publishing

Layout: Allan Tépper

Covers, spine and back cover: Andreína Ascanio Toro

ISBN of the printed soft cover version:

979-8-9909036-2-3

ISBN of the electronic version (ebook):

979-8-9909036-3-0

In honor of my husband who died 15 years ago, October 8, 2008, my children and grandchildren.

1

MY CHILDHOOD AND FAMILY

I was born on February 16, 1940 in Alia, Giardino di Palermo, Italy. I am the daughter of Vincenzo Di Sclafani and Giuseppina Blanda. My father and mother married in 1931. At that time, my father was 24 years old and my mother was 18 years old.

My grandparents were:

- Lucio Orfanello, maternal grandfather.
- Agada De Orfanello, maternal grandmother.
- Gaetano Di Sclafani, paternal grandfather.
- Rosalia Lopresti, paternal grandmother.

My parents had 7 children and I was the third of my siblings. I was very smart as a child. I inherited it from my dad.

When I was 2 years old, my dad went to war and came back when I was 3 years old. He brought me a doll that had straw in its belly. In the house where we lived, we had a dining room upstairs with a round table and I would go around the table with my doll.

My grandparents on my mother's side lived across the street. You had to go around the corner to go next door, where there was a parking lot owned by Aunt Nucasa. My mother was sick with malaria. At that time there was a lot of sickness.

Since it was wartime, the rich people from Palermo came to the town, which was safer. One of them was Mrs. Pierina, who came with her whole family. The bombs sounded above the houses and we hid where my grandfather's mule ate. The houses at that time had walls one meter wide, doors and windows with big and thick bars, because we had to watch out for the mafia.

In 1945, the war ended and the US-American soldiers stayed in Palermo, because they had sent their sons and grandsons to war. There was a party with music, singing, and food. The beach in Mondello was the best beach. The soldiers paraded in the villages and we on the national roads said «hello, hello» and they gave us candies and chocolates in green trucks.

When the war ended, Mrs. Pierina went to Palermo and the grandchildren started a carpentry shop. They were the grandchildren of aunt Nucasa. Giuseppe was serious, handsome, small and cheerful. I would go with my doll and he would make the bed for her, another day the chair or the table. He always pleased me, but first I had to give him kisses and hugs. I was the most loved child in the neighborhood and everyone hugged and kissed me.

There was only one doctor, Doctor Gucciones from Palermo. He and his wife had no children and were very rich people. When I passed by, the wife would tell me to come upstairs and give me candy.

In front of my father's house lived uncle Pino, who was born in that house. There were 10 squares where we played, 5 on one side and 5 on the other side, and you had to jump without falling. We played politics, one group was for the monarchy and the other was democratic. I was always democratic: None of my family was of different politics and neither was my husband.

There were also uncle Masi's games, like tug-of-war that had to be done with thick thread. Four points from above in the mouth, on the side of the arms and below another girl.

Once the war was over, Mussolini, a black-shirt socialist, entered. You had to go to the square to sing and exercise and the children of his party were called *Balilla*. Mussolini put an end to the Mafia or made them go into hiding and sent the King into exile. He modified all of Italy, but he put the rich in charge and the villages were backward. In the villages there was no water, plumbing or electricity for many years.

My dad made pipes that went under a bridge. At that time, there were *cántaros*, as they used to be called. They were very tall and the women would put them on their heads and then throw them far away. There was a waterspout near the bridge and my dad would go to the water trough with two mules and bring water for drinking and cooking. For cleaning and washing, there was a well.

My mother was a very homely woman, who didn't even go outside to call the vendors. My dad would buy everything from them on time so he didn't have to move around. When I grew a little more, she would send me to pay the taxes with my grandmother and we would leave at 2 a.m. We would arrive at the place, which was a family house, and we would go to bed, since we had to wait for the morning.

There were some doctors who came every Wednesday and two graduated midwives. The doctors were Dr. Scialaba, Dr. Cartabillotta and Dr. Barcellona. Doctor Cartabillotta was cheerful and helpful. He had four brothers, all tall. When he graduated, he had a girlfriend close to the house. They would kiss and we would run them off. He would go to the patients' homes, but it didn't last long because he became a dentist and did very well. Sadly he died young and left two sons, a doctor and an engineer.

In the past, barbers used to pull teeth and cut hair, and everything was paid for with grain. At the end of the year, women had their hair cut.

My great-grandfather studied to become a priest, but I don't know why he stopped studying. He worked for 40 years in the post office, where he worked as a banker, telegram and postman. My mother used to tell me that my grandfather used to tell them:

«Go to Mass and do not enter the sacristy.»

He had four daughters and two sons, one of whom died. He would immediately bring telegrams to the families the same night and say that they were waiting for him. It was wartime. He died before I walked and left a name to my grandfather.

His dad went to New York in 1906 and the petitions at that time were made in September 1903. He left on a ship full of the surrounding towns and we have a chart with all the names and the manifest. He left four children, but one died. He was well loved.

My grandmother was left with one daughter and 6 sons. My grandmother withdrew her children from school, including my dad, who had started third grade but could not continue. My grandmother married off all the children, well married and with lots of partying. She was a very brave woman and I resemble her.

Eventually, all the children married and we formed a family of 32 married cousins. There were 64 of us and to have a party and you didn't need guests. Every year there were 31 parties and carnivals. We always ate all together and dad knew how to keep the whole family together.

When we were at my grandmother's house, pasta and sauce were cooked and we ate where the bread was kneaded. Sadly she died on August 8, 1953, when I was 13 years old. Her blood pressure was rising and he got a lot of paralysis, but at that time the only cure was to draw blood.

My grandfather Damaniano Blanda was born in 1880 and died in 1964. The night he died I dreamed about him. My grandmother was a very elegant woman and at that time, she wore gloves, a short jacket and a small heel. She was born in 1890 and died in 1972, but I saw her in 1971.

2

MY SCHOOL

School was up to fifth grade and you had to go to high school in Lercara. There were no vehicles and you had to look for a residence there. I was very little and my father would not have sent me. In the town they built a very modern school up to sixth grade, with a dining room.

When I was 6 years old, I went to school. I had a very pretty teacher who came from Palermo and painted herself. I would pick her up and drop her off and she would give me a picture with a crucifix to put in the school. In third grade, she told me she didn't know if she was coming back and I started crying. I said:

«I don't want the painting, I want you back.»

She came back to fifth grade.

When the war was over, a communiqué came out to make a theme about the Italian reconstructions. I did it, but I went to my uncle Pino and asked him to modify it. But first, I had to give him hugs and kisses and then he told me that it was okay, that if he did them they would reject it. They sent me a package of chocolate.

School at that time was tough. In first grade they gave us addition, subtraction and division and in first grade I was the best in math and history. I remember *My Broken Doll*, *Story of a Piece of Bread* and *Story of a Tree*, which I saw in every classroom.

Today there is a bus that goes to Lercara and people wait for them until they return, a well maintained World War II bus to Morrocoy.

3

THE AFTERMATH OF THE WAR
MY GRANDFATHER

The Sicilians traveled to New York in 1906. They did not know how to eat or speak. They had to save and, working pick and shovel, were able to buy a house, land and cattle. Unfortunately they were called up for World War I in 1915 until 1918. In 1917 a cousin died in Padua. Two years ago, I went to Padua; a general took us where my grandfather fought, where he fell and where he was buried. A cousin of my grandfather's came back without a leg from the war. My dad made me meet them and those are the memories we have.

The last one to die was my uncle Gaetano, who went to war for seven years and died at the age of 93. When he came back, he passed by my maternal grandmother's house and carried me all the way up the plain where my grandmother Lilla lived, to where my mother lived. When the neighbors saw them, they said to her:

«Put it down, it's too heavy.»

and they called my grandmother. I remember she came out, knelt down and kissed the earth. My grandmother Lilla lived to be 93 years old.

Then came my uncle Salvatore, who went to war for 5 years. The Germans took him prisoner and they were going to kill him. The Germans were very bad, because they did World War I and World War II. They were real murderers. Fortunately a counter-order came and they released him in that cellar. There he got sick with rheumatism and was never cured. He was the husband of my mother's sister, my aunt Maria. I remember that they took my sister Lina all night long, but she did not want to go and cried.

The last one to arrive was my uncle, my mother's brother. So many times they told my grandmother that he was coming. We traveled 3 kilometers to wait for him and he never arrived. Finally, after 7 years, he arrived. It was *Bersaglieri* and he had a picture with his hat with many feathers. He came like everyone else, without clothes and shoes, because that's how the Italians were left in the war. He brought two rolls of cloth that he used to get married and a bracelet for the bride. I remember that they started the courtship with lots of flowers and partying and got married soon after. I was seated in front of them because my uncle was my christening godfather.

Those were very sad times. Today, nobody wants war, because it means economic disaster and death.

4

MY YOUTH

In my time, there was no study, but young people were sent to prepare themselves. I went to learn embroidery from my sister Lina. She was the best dressmaker in high fashion. Some knew how to machine embroider and today young people only want to study.

In 1950, my mother set up the loom and later, in the spring, I went with her to bleach it. Water was poured on them every so often and they were embroidered, making towels, sheets and bedspreads. She divided them among the seven children. My father read by candlelight. Every book he read, he would repeat it from the first page to the last. He was very smart. In my family, I came out like him.

I had many admirers at that time. A boy would pass by and then stand on the corner and say that I was the prettiest girl in town. Together with my grandfather on my mother's side, we used to go out to a piece of land he had nearby to pick roses and mint. There was land where a boy lived who would pass by on horseback and would get off to greet my grandfather, who would say:

«When I'm alone he doesn't greet me.»

My grandfather was my friend and many times we sat on the balcony to talk. He gave me a lot of advice and told me that this boy was no good and that I was too small. One memory I have of my grandfather: He was sitting on a step crying the day I got married, because he had lost his granddaughter and friend.

5

MY HUSBAND, SALVATORE

My husband's name was Salvatore Nasca Orfanello and he was my mother's cousin. I became his girlfriend in 1958, when I was 18 years old, and it was not easy. I had two older sisters, one 22 and the other 20. Salvatore had left for Venezuela in 1951 and his father had left in 1950.

He worked hard and did all kinds of work in the village, mainly iron with the forge. At that time, everything was done with beaten iron. I remember he made the grating on the church of Santa Ana and he made the mule and horse irons. There was nothing he didn't know how to do well, like putting the mules and horses on the floor. It was a technique he worked on a lot. When he arrived in Venezuela he worked with construction and mechanics. A man gave him a job as a mechanic and he worked 18 hours a day.

He retired earning something and bought a pickup truck, with which he went to Caracas, buying cookies and candies. At that time a business would buy a pack of candy from him, but then there was no sale. Then he bought a little 350 truck that he paid off in 6 months. He went everywhere, all the way to Pico El Águila in the state of Mérida. In 54 he went racing with a modified Studebaker car.

Little by little, he bought 13 trucks and had 13 salesmen. He would go to Caracas to buy the merchandise wholesale. The fall of General Pérez Jiménez in 58 was very serious. The Europeans left, people were left owing him and there was less purchasing power. He was losing a lot of money. He had worked a lot and suffered from nerves, so much so that he could not eat. A cousin took him to Caracas to a doctor, where he talked a lot until he could not take it anymore and made a gesture of exhaustion. The doctor told him:

«I know what you need: a vacation, far away.»

His father paid his fare for 3 months and he went to Italy. He arrived at my grandmother's house, his mother's sister, and my grandmother invited all the children. One had no children, another had three and lived far away, my uncle had two boys and my mother had seven. While I was eating, he remembered me and I remembered him. I remember my dad always talked about him. My aunt and godmother died when I was 11 years old, Salvatore carried the urn all the way to the cemetery.

He went on a trip with a cousin and they traveled all over Europe. Even a German singer joined them and some fellow countrymen who were in Milan. He forgot everything; he had that character. A friend called them saying that they were going to get the mandatory military ballot and came to talk to my dad. My grandfather refused. I told them I wanted him and my dad told him to come at night. He had three days left.

We had the round table downstairs and the third night he told them he hadn't looked me in the face. My dad laughed. While at the blacksmith's, he met a man from Palermo who had been hunting. He liked to go hunting but what he killed was picked up by others. He told that man that he was going to confirm them.

The next day we went to Palermo, with all my family and cousins. He wanted to kiss me but I didn't know and he told me he didn't know what to think about me. I cried, he wiped my tears and I kept the handkerchief. On the next trip he wrote me a letter which I kept. The letters took a long time to arrive and then he began sending them via registered mail.

He proposed a civil marriage so I could get my passport. We went with my mother to the Council and my mother stayed outside. The attorney attended me and asked me:

«Young lady, do you know what you are doing?»

I asked him why and he told me that if I got married by civil ceremony, he would have me married in the sacristy. I wrote to Salvatore and he answered that we were getting married by proxy. My father did not like that proposal and even less my grandfather, because he said:

«What if he doesn't come?»

Dad wrote, guaranteeing that he was coming. My grandfather repeated:

«What if he doesn't come?»

and I replied:

«I'm leaving.»

At that time, the church marriage was together with the civil marriage. He sent the power of attorney to my father and I got married on August 22, 1959. All my mother's family knew about it, because they were at home every day. My dad's family didn't know. The parish priest published it but he didn't understand it.

He wrote a letter saying he was coming on the 22nd and never arrived. Aunt Marieta told me that the plane had been delayed somewhere. He arrived on the 26th, he had stayed in Milan to make several dresses. When he arrived, my brothers came to tell him. I didn't speak. I didn't go out. I was sick with nerves and I couldn't speak.

The next day, we went to Palermo to buy everything. They had to go back to town to see where they could have the party and it was held at my father's house, since he had a big house. My father told Mrs. Nuncia that he was waiting for me and she told them that she was sleeping with her children.

Finally, the day of the wedding party arrived, November 7. Father Gibino said in the sermon that the Church had collaborated with us, but no one understood him. After the party, my husband grabbed me and took me to the national road. My dad, when he did not see me, came and said:

«You stole my daughter from me.»

We arrived in Palermo to a 5 star hotel. I was dressed as a bride. We left on a trip and returned on the 21st. Before returning, he took me to Palermo to the doctor and said that before three months I'd be pregnant.

We left on the 22nd to Palermo, with all my family, uncles, aunts, uncles and cousins. When the godfather, who had confirmed it, saw the weeping that was going to form, he grabbed me and took me up on the ship. He climbed on the other side and we arrived in Naples, and then began the trip to Venezuela.

6

EMIGRATING TO VENEZUELA

We left on the ship Venezuela on November 22, 1959. It was a very difficult trip for me because I got seasick. There was a jukebox where my husband put 100 liras and played the song *La Malagueña* and other songs that he always requested to sing.

We went through Tenerife and it was very nice. He told me he would buy me a big doll, but he didn't remember. He bought me a shawl. Then we went through Port-au-Prince and a lot of people came up smelling like savages, dressed in pink, blue and white. I was hiding, because I was afraid and felt very bad. He was playing with two children and liked to play with them. I would stay downstairs, crying. He was mortified.

I was afraid, I didn't like it upstairs or downstairs. Sometimes I slept downstairs with him. There was a lady to whom he told that I was pregnant and the lady told him that it was bad for me to bathe every day and he told me that until I arrived in Venezuela not to bathe.

On December 7, we arrived at the port of La Guaira and the family came to pick us up. I felt very bad. I remembered my family and cried.

In Barquisimeto, Venezuela I got a real family: My father José Ángel Briceño and his wife María Luz, who gave me a lot of advice. After a few years, I lost my father Briceño, on April 4, 1975; my father Motta on August 8, 77; my father on December 24, 79; my mother Luz in 1980 and my mother Modesta, who was next to the farm, in 1985.

7

MY SONS, ANTONIO AND VINCENZO, ARE BORN

I became pregnant and my son Antonio was born on September 15, 1960, weighing 5.4 kg. When he was born, I was thinking about my family. I had a miscarriage at the age of 23. It was a girl. It was St. Joseph's Day and I cried a lot. I was very upset.

I had surgery at the age of 23 for appendicitis. The doctor the next day told me that the last word I said was that Doctor José Gregorio Hernández would help me. I told them I was devoted to the Doctor and he told me he had a small clinic with that name.

After that, I could not go out pregnant and I felt very sick, from 9 o'clock at night until 5 o'clock in the morning, but I could work without any problem. Dr. Martín Ibarra attended me at that time and did all the tests. He told me that we were fine. One day he said to me:

«Tell Salvatore that there is a center for spiritualists.»

He was a Mason and his religion was Spiritualism. I was attended by a friend of my husband's about the same age. He came to open the door and my husband asked him:

«Do you believe in this?»

and I answered him:

«I didn't believe before, but now I believe.»

I was seen by him because he was known to be known to my husband, Salvatore. Salvatore came in with me and asked him if I had my tests done. He replied that everything was fine. He turned into a doctor of hundreds of years and said when he sits on the couch, you can see.

My husband wouldn't take me, so I went with my father-in-law and sister-in-law. I was not working. There was a child that a spirit was trying to join and could not. There was a child and he started talking to the child in a strange language. I didn't go anymore.

One early morning, at 4 a.m., my husband says to me:

«I'm going out to find Ismael to go on a trip.»

I went to sleep in the lower part of the bed and Dr. José Gregorio Hernández accompanied me to sleep. When my husband arrived, I told him and he answered that I had dreamed it. I became pregnant with my other son and my husband left on a trip on the 27th, the day I was 9 months pregnant. My son Vincenzo was born on August 31 and weighed 6 kg. It was a very bad delivery, with too much suffering. When he was born, he didn't cry at first, but he was spanked and then he cried.

When Enzo was one year old, he developed a very high fever and died at midnight. I implored Dr. José Gregorio Hernández with great courage. I was 27 years old and had a dead child in my arms. At 12:30, he revived and we went to the Calicanto Clinic. He had a fever of 43 degrees Celsius, so they put him in a tub of ice and water. The next day he had sores in his mouth.

My son studied at Colegio San Pedro. When he arrived there was María, who worked with me for four years and then went to learn to sew. I used to get up at 4 o'clock in the morning to make lunch. With her I had no problem, because she did the cooking, washing, ironing and cleaning. She studied down the block at Paul School. On Saturday her two sisters and her father would come and then leave.

8

OUR WORK

I n 1968 my husband won a bidding process with Vencemos, a cement producer in Venezuela. My husband didn't want to take me, because he said I wasn't used to it. As I always carried a card in my pocket, I called a lady who owned a hotel and restaurant and she helped me rent the house. I called the driver, Domingo Mujica, and told him to come in. He loaded the little I had in the room: the bed, the crib, the sewing machine (because I had been sewing for a long time).

My husband didn't want to and started yelling that he wouldn't take me, but I insisted that I wouldn't stay. We left early and at midnight he told me he was going to Vencemos to see if there was a car. I stayed outside, I was afraid. There was a scary mango tree and the drivers were coming and going like dogs in their own house.

We were deprived of everything, even food. I told a driver, Felipe Espinosa, to take me to buy fabric to make curtains. We went right away. I made the curtains and put them on. I didn't go more than a few days and my husband had to leave for Puerto La Cruz to do some work at the La Vergareña Ranch, near Brazil. I was left alone with the white and gray cement work all the way to Caracas, the plaster from Puerto La Cruz and clinker from Maracaibo. I was afraid and when we went to bed in the office. I put the file and the desk behind the door.

We worked with affiliates. We were buying cars and paying a lot of interest and he helped me with the affiliates. The 5% I charged was quite a lot of money at that time, about US$3,500 a month.

The work we were doing was very cheap. One day from Caracas they sent 5 bolivars for a raise, but Dr. Useche gave them to him alive and gave us 2. My husband told me and one day I told the driver of the van:

«Leo, we are going to Vencemos.»

I got dressed up nicely and met Mr. Cameo, the plant manager and a sincere friend. I asked him where Dr. Useche was and he took me to the door. He had an eight-seat airplane and a race car. I did not sit down. I told him he was a thief, a man without scruples, with the percentage he earned with the three plants he could steal enough, to watch the combat movies to see how the drivers arrived broken, tired. The soldiers arrived naked and without shoes, and so did the drivers.

We paid them 18%, averaged on Sunday and 60 days of benefits. Eugenio Mendoza is also a thief. My husband told me that Cameo saw me at Vencemos and I told him that he did not answer me and that the work was too cheap. He also couldn't control all the companies they had and they were being robbed of workers. The only one they had left was Vencemos and they had a fatal heart attack. My father was very sick with cancer in his lungs. My thought was that if Eugenio Mendoza had died, my father could likely die too.

After 25 long years in the transportation business, the plant had closed down in the sale of trucks. I had 223 thousand bolivars in the bank book. We got a 7,500-meter plot of land on the entire avenue of the Industrial Zone. We borrowed 200 thousand bolivars from the bank and bought it for 415 thousand bolivars. I had 8 thousand left. When I went to see my dad the last time, I bought the ticket.

The owner was from Rome and we made drafts to pay them every 3 months. He returned it to remove some constructions from the land and only made the floor, the sheds, four offices and an apartment below. Four stores were built with the sale of trucks and loans to the bank and everyone congratulated my husband for the overhang he made, 8 meters deep and 60 meters long. All the people who passed by looked at it.

One day we went to spend the day with the Chamber of Transportation and several carriers were there. Mr. Perucho Saldivia knew that my dad was very ill and brought us a cake for 19 years of marriage. My husband had bought two sheep, another one brought wine and whiskey. Mr. Rincón talked to me and said:

«If he doesn't win it, it'll be a tie.»

Mr. Manrique told them:

> «Mrs. Nasca knows more about transportation than we do.»

Every night, I would start to make working relationships. The next door neighbor, Mr. Mustafa who had a business on the corner, would say to me:

> «Neighbor, all night that machine makes noise.»

The accounting also came out of that machine, which was 6 months younger than I, from July 16, 1941. A lot of taxes were paid with the transport.

At one point during those years, we were not working because of the national union and a boy came to ask me for a job. I told him we were not working and he insisted. I told him I had the washing upstairs and he started washing, but he had never worked. He pointed the hose at the electricity and got electrocuted. I was watching and suddenly saw him lying down. I went over to him. I saw that the hose was pouring water on him and I took it away. The electricity went through his hands and came out through his testicles. I ran to the bakery and the Portuguese guy ran out. I went to the pharmacy and the pharmacist came with me. Then the ambulance came and picked him up.

The mother came and I couldn't speak. All I could do was sob. The pharmacist told me:

«I'm afraid for you.»

That was true. I was very concerned. At that moment my son Enzo came. We went to the lawyer, a friend, Esteban Duarte. I asked him if we had a serious problem and he told me to wait, that at that moment the serious thing was the night. My husband, who was in Caracas, came and I went to the family's house. I was afraid. I did not want to go, but he told me that I had to show my face. Well, his father came to meet him, hugging him and saying:

«God called them. He needs them.»

He said that the expenses were on us. It was 15 thousand bolivars that we didn't have. On Sunday, we went to my brother-in-law's house. We told him and he gave me the check, which we paid him after 2 years. He had a dark-haired brother who was dark like him and every time I saw him, my blood ran high.

I wore out my feet with transportation. I spent 25 years in transportation and 27 years managing the business with truck parts, I wore out my back and knee. I had knee surgery in 2012 and 2013, full prosthesis, and my back also with full prosthesis.

9

THE MASONS

One day my dad Briceño tells my husband: «Read this bill.»

He passed it to me and told him that he was good to be a Mason. He was from St. Martín de Porres.

There we met Dr. Motta, the hospital pathologist and professor of the last year of medicine. The son of rich people, his mother had died when he was 3 years old and his father was a civil engineer. He bought a theater because he liked the dancer. His father told him to study engineering and he replied: «I will study medicine.»

When he graduated, he insisted that he study engineering, but he did not respond. He left for Venezuela married with a daughter and a belly. He had married

Mrs. Ucha, from Trieste. She was not Catholic and became Catholic to marry him.

Her father had a navy that the government expropriated during wartime. Later, when it was recovered, she and her brother sold it and she bought a very big shiny one. Motta never talked about Caripito. Mrs. Ucha said that people chewed and smoked tobacco. She lived in one room and suffered from heart disease and I never asked her how they got to Barquisimeto.

They had a very old car and one Sunday a Fiat sales manager came to the house. My husband called them and bought the car for cash because he liked it. Consuelo studied in México and had two children, a boy and a girl. The boy she left and the girl she brought with her. Cristina studied anthropology and did post-graduate studies in France. Cristina had three boys. She was married to an Argentinean, a Pinochet fanatic and they divorced. I have as a souvenir of her a *bombonera* that she brought me.

After sixteen years, my husband was made a 33rd degree Mason. He would go to Caracas and take me to the banquets, where he was very elegant. Mr. Camin Plana, a Mason and great friend, was proud to be from Catalonia and always gave me a bouquet of flowers. There was an 85 year old man in San Martín who used to make a speech to me.

In 1974, Carlos Andrés Pérez left power. The Masons had the disposition to promote my husband from colonel to general. To authorize my husband, he had to be studied. It was a Saturday and I arrived home with my son Enzo, who was 8 years old, in his underwear and he said that this child had a good future. When they made him a general, he sent my husband a special card.

One Holy Week we had to go to the pool. I bought a bathing suit, glasses and a dress, all fancy, but we didn't go to the pool, we went to the party. He led the party with his hat at the entrance. My husband took his place with the Masons and I sat with Camin Plana's daughter. She was a year younger than I and a pediatrician. They got me drunk on Don Perignon champagne. Her husband, also a pediatrician, was tired, but she said, «If Mrs. Nasca doesn't leave, I'm not leaving.»

Finally, we two inebriated women left. We stayed in a five-star hotel.

I told my dad Motta that I was going to collaborate with the Masons and outside a young man would give them a thermos of coffee and a cake. When I didn't have time, I called Cinlita, a second year medical student. With the income, I covered the minor expenses until the business was over. I called my father Motta and told him that the business was over and on Friday he brought me 1000 lottery tickets, at 10 bolivars each. I took some of them to friends who had businesses and I sold the rest myself. We made 3700 bolivars and he gave me all the profit.

One day we went to Maracay and I went to see Doctor Martín Ibarra, but my husband did not want to come. The Doctor lived in Las Delicias and was 90 years old. He told me that I would have been a great seer. I think that with time and experience I am more than a clairvoyant.

10

MY CHILDREN AND
GRANDCHILDREN

M y son Enzo enrolled in mechanical engineering, but the university was closed for a long time and he did not want to study anymore. One day I took him to Doctor Orellana and in the hallway of the Polyclinic I was crying so much that the tears reached the floor. I went in and told him, crying, that Enzo did not want to study. He told him that there were many careers in the future and convinced him to enroll in computer engineering.

«I'm going to science school.»

he said.

In 1992 he graduated *summa cum laude* and made his speech at St. Francis Church. He was the first one and when he went up to the stage everyone shouted in one voice with the family. It was a party with 120 graduates and everyone was congratulating me. We were happy and felt very proud as parents.

I wanted him to work with a transnational company. His professors had a company and invited him to go work there. After a while, he told me he didn't like it. He went the next day and looked for the professor to tell him that he was not going anymore. The third day he went and he wasn't there.

«I'm not coming anymore.»

He went to work in the parts company.

My son Toni got engaged to a girl he had known for 20 years. They got married in Caracas in 1992. She got pregnant after 2 months and wanted him to annul the marriage. They threatened him in front of us. My son told them:

«If I hadn't had a business, you wouldn't have married me. It belongs to my parents. I studied for 10 years.»

The father was a bad guy from Rome, a sorcerer who filled them with witchcraft. They went to the Corp-banca bank and the bank's answer was that he had nothing. We were able to see our granddaughter when Toni was granted shared parental rights. My son told them that he wanted his daughter, Melani, and I had to give her education, clothes and maintenance. We saw her when she was 9 years old. She was given a watch and a telephone and they took it away.

A lady who was a Rosicrucian extracted all the witch-craft out of him with a heavy pot. He won the divorce and if he had wanted to, the Pope would have annulled their marriage in the church, but he had no one in sight to marry. He then married Carmen Elena in 2000. They lasted three and a half years and then he divorced her. She was a very educated girl. She did not want to have children but she did want to bring up her sister's son.

Then he lived with Ángela, a daughter of Italians and Spaniards. The daughter he had was tremendous. She made them believe that she would give him a son and made him take her to the doctor, but it was a lie. She thought about going to Miami to hire a company with a court and a lawyer. She called me when she had knee surgery. She got a sham divorce. She told her dad she was going with the boyfriend to a party and the dad said,

«Come early.»

«When I have sores on my feet.»

The younger brother had been killed in an accident and the father had a bad liver.

I sold a luxury townhouse for that child. Thank God he was born well, at 5 o'clock in the morning. I spent a year and a half taking care of him and he still remembers. He was 75 years old, suffered from thyroid and could not take it anymore. He is now 8 years old, almost a black belt and very intelligent. My husband was not lucky enough to see grandchildren, but the neighbor had a granddaughter and that was our granddaughter. We would arrive tired and start playing with Paola.

My son Enzo got married at 41. She was 35 when she got pregnant. They had a luncheon to communicate that she was pregnant and my husband was in tears, but he was not lucky enough to meet him. Sadly my husband died on October 8, 2008, before the child was born.

They spent New Year's Eve in Acarigua. The father's mother and brother began to say that in Venezuela there were Cuban doctors who killed people, that they were bad. The son left for Acarigua and did not want to return. She called him all the time and told them:

«At 7 months I'll let you know.»

but never did. He traveled four times a year for the residency with a good pocket, the best hotels and the best restaurants. I told them the baby was not going to be born in Venezuela, but in the United States. The first child was born on April 16, 2009 at 4 o'clock in the afternoon. The second one, on December 9, 2010 at 4 o'clock in the afternoon. She wanted a cesarean section and the doctor was working until Thursday.

Salvatore Jesús is 14 years and 6 months old. Enzo José is 13 years old. The little one, Salvatore Antonio, is 8 years old and was born on September 3, 2015. With the three grandchildren, I am very happy and all three are very smart. Enzito wants to study Robotics Engineering, Salvatore Jesús has not defined himself and Salvatore Antonio says he is going to work with his dad, although sometimes he says he wants to be President. His father tells him that if he does not study, he will send him to the military.

I was widowed at the age of 68. My husband died because his circulation did not reach his head and he did not take his pills. This is the sad story, because the family is each to his own and I spend 8 hours a day alone. At night I am alone, watching TV in the library.

11

SOME MIRACLES

I have received several miracles. I met Monsignor
Chuao. He was Portuguese and had spent many
years in Poland with Pope John Paul II and had 60
years of psychology studies. He came to Barquisimeto,
built the church and with his right arm, he healed
people. Mrs. Asunción, a Portuguese woman, arrived
earlier and sat next to him. When I arrived, she called
me Asunción:

«This post belongs to Mrs. Teresa.»

When she turned 94 years old, a party was held for her.
Chávez' wife, the dictator, came with a person who
worked at Promar and they offered her a cake. She
came saying she wanted spiritual counseling. I told the
Monsignor and he got angry. She did not want to eat
the cake they offered.

One Sunday, I had severe back pain and tearfully told my husband to take me to the Monsignor. He told me that the nephew had come to pick him up. On Sunday, we went to the airport. We rushed there and he was gone, he had gone inside. Before Christmas I called him and found out he was in an old people's home, I passed the phone to my husband and he was happy. In January he died.

For years I had gone with my husband to say the Rosary. When we started it was just the two of us. After a week, we couldn't fit on the plain.

One day we were going to Maracay to see my husband's family. I spent the 23rd making food and on the 24th we were leaving. We forgot about the food and left it in the hallway and we realized when we were 100 km away. I called Mr. Hidalgo to go get the food and eat it. When I returned, my neighbor told me that it was a miracle because Hidalgo was not working, neither he nor his wife.

In 2004, I spoke with the Director of Sports, President Caldera. The first trip was to Perú. He saw a Nasca advertisement on a T-shirt and brought it to me. He said to me:

«A small gift.»

I told him that for me it is a great gift and I keep it as a souvenir.

One day I arrived at the airport at dawn, tired. A young man about 25 years old came up to me and said:

«Lie down, you are very tired.»

I told him I was afraid and he took the books out of his backpack, put them under my head, then put the paletot on top of me and sat next to me. When the plane was about to leave, he said to me:

«The plane is going to leave.»

I said:

«My guardian angel, when shall we meet?»

He answered that he did not know. Some boys started to say that in the early morning, rats came out. The young man went to get a couch and a chair and said that he was taking care of the rats. He woke me up and I went out.

These are all miracles that I have received. I am an international Rotarian, a Rotarian at heart. For more than 50 years I have helped children and the elderly, collecting clothes, food, toys, bringing happiness to poor homes. I feel happy.

I had a closet 100 km away where I collected clothes for others. I used to go on Saturdays from 3 to 7, in a garage with zinc sheets, but after a long time they took the place away from me. Here in the United States, I do the same thing and I work with Latinos and indigenous people. Anglo-Americans and Puerto Ricans do not open their doors and do not give anything. For the earthquake in Turkey, I sent two big loads and for the hurricane in Orlando I sent another one. Now I always pick them up and bring them close to the house, where trucks leave every day.

12

MOST RECENT VISIT TO VENEZUELA

At the beginning of November, I had to travel for 14 days to Venezuela, but I could only stay for 8 days, after 9 years without going. Arriving in Caracas, I went to the Eurobuilding Hotel, where they charged me US$200 for lodging and US$50 for food. In the morning I went to the airport and they told me that the plane was going to leave, but it was more than an hour and a half away. A young lady showed me in, but told me that the ticket was for the next day and that it was no good. I told her that I wanted to redo the ticket and she said no. I went to the La Bandera bus terminal and bought the bus ticket for US$8. There was a young woman who was going to Barquisimeto and I told her to go around to see if she could get a car. She told me there was one with 3 passengers missing and I told her I would pay for them.

We arrived in Barquisimeto and when I was dropped off at the house, I saw that I had forgotten the keys. I called a locksmith, but I couldn't wait because I was in a rush. They called others, who opened the door with a wire and charged me US$450. When I arrived, I fought 3 hours with locksmiths, calling them thieves, that they had stolen my money. They didn't give me anything back. The neighbor who had helped me was shocked. I felt calmer at home than at the hotel.

I went to the hotel which used to be 5 stars and the neighbor asked me why I didn't stay. I told him I felt more at ease in the hotel. They charged me US$40 cash for the whole night. I had no milk or chamomile tea and they made a small breakfast. I lost 5 kg in a few days.

The next day I had to pick up my dead husband's document, with which I had to transfer the apartment to the youngest of my grandchildren. The man told me to give him US$200 and in less than half an hour I had the document. There were many dollar thieves and he took me wherever he went, hugging me, as if I were his mother.

I had to clean the apartment and Rosita cleaned it. We filled 12 black bags that my son sent me, with folders and catalogs. I gave the caretaker $30. I emptied the entire apartment and made two piles, one for Rosita and one for the driver. I gave them pots, a grill, sheets, towels, cushions, shoes, everything there was. The man has a 2 year old child and I gave him a motorcycle and three dolls that belonged to my grandson and he told me that the child was happy with the motorcycle.

I lived in a rented house for 4 years and 6 years in the farmhouse in front of the medical school. There were boys who had no food and no fare, and they sold me their books, which I always bought from them. I made a library 3.50 by 2.70 meters. There were some books in the house that I had never looked at, until that moment when I cleaned the apartment. I saw the Francisco de Miranda book, which had been in the house for 50 years and I had never looked at it, and other books. When I arrived, I saw an alternative book for healing. The mother of the cardiac doctor and my neighbor were losing mass. There were six pages that talked about it and I sent the information to both of them and they were cured. In another case of another person, the letter did not arrive and he died.

I went to Caracas and the driver who brought my things charged me US$40. I was carrying all my husband's photos, diplomas, books and all his 33rd Grade badges. I ran out of money. The man who did the race for me went around to get a spot until he finally got it, cashed out and gave me US$20. I finally arrived in Orlando with a lot of bitterness and met my grandson and my family.

With all the badges I brought from Freemasonry, my 8 year old grandson put all those memories well organized by year and with the portrait of *Nonno* (grandfather) Salvatore Antonio. He believes in his *Nonno* and says he looks just like him. Yesterday he sent him five balloons and watched them until they disappeared. None of the other two remember him and of the grandchildren, only Salvatore Antonio always talks about the *Nonno*.

13

RECENT EVENTS

This is my story. I am happy now. I am healthy and I am 84 years old. I have a cardiologist-surgeon who loves me and I am going to give him my body when I die. He has to transplant my heart. I have a young Italian-Venezuelan cardiologist who gave me a bypass. I call him «my fatso». He is more than 2 meters tall and plump. He has a very nice family: his father, his mother and two daughters, one who is studying medicine and the other is 14 years old, besides a 4 year old boy. I have an immunologist who loves me and treats me well. I don't know the cardiologist's daughter, but I love her like I love Paola. She is 17 years old and is studying law.

I cannot go to Miami to deliver this book, because I had a problem with the rental of the rooms. I paid US$51 in condo maintenance. They had to pay and told me to go to a lawyer. Yesterday I went and the contract was never valid, because they rented for the church and put 200 children with notice and everything. He has paid US$95,000 and if he wants to stay, he has to pay US$40,000. Because of his cowardice, I have closed my life with this last event.

May God protect me. I made two rosaries to Blessed José Gregorio Hernández to cure Mr. David Bello Trinidad, a young man of 30 years old. He was going to pay his taxes, he looked at me and said:

«I was looking at you, your calmness and kindness.»

I grabbed a policeman by the arm and told him:

«Taxes. I don't speak English.»

and a lady immediately paid the tax on my behalf.

Even a war was paid for with kindness and tranquility.

ABOUT THE AUTHOR AND HER OTHER WORKS

Teresa Di Sclafani De Nasca was born in Italy. She has also lived in Venezuela and the United States.

Before publishing this Diary, she had published

The World According to Teresa Di Sclafani in three languages, with its three versions:

- Audiobook
- Electronic book
- Printed book

For more information on these versions of

The World According to Teresa Di Sclafani, visit

TheworldaccordingtoTeresa.com. It is also listed in two other languages (Italian and Castilian, aka «Spanish», as indicated on that website.